Crying Choruses

DeAndrea Jordan

BookLeaf Publishing

Presentation by *BookLeaf Publishing*

Web: www.bookleafpub.com

E-mail: info@bookleafpub.com

ISBN: 9789357697026

First edition 2023

DEDICATION

To the old me, Beware.

ACKNOWLEDGEMENT

I thank the Universe. I thank Catherine and George for life. I thank the other George and Mattie for giving me life. I thank Tristan for the hugs in the rain. I thank the nameless naked man for the pain. I thank Eastside of San Antonio for molding me. I thank UTOTO for scolding me. I thank Yen for being my sister. I thank my siblings for giving me chances to be a sister. I thank my temporary Dillard buddies for helping me navigate the system. I thank Henry for making me want more. I thank the others for reminding me not to trust. I thank Alvin for telling the truth with a smile and keeping me safe. I thank Jacob for gifting me life. I thank those gifts, J'Andre and Jada, for saving my life. I thank Ms Valdez for accepting me. I thank Fred for helping me flee. I thank Jesse for awakening me.

PREFACE

This was finally written to prove its existence. Proof that I was capable of facing my real thoughts in black and white without falling to pieces. Perhaps those who read this will breathe in its truth.

Pick One

We are not the same.

I laugh while you cry
Smirk as you ask why.

I love to lose instead of
being loose with love.

Bye! I exclaim as I plan to remain in my lane.

I refrain from a state of mad
while you complain how life is sad.

We...
Me...
I...
am not the same...

The old me vs. new me
Which one is actually sane?

Fix it

Crusty memories of love,
lust, and admiration
shattered all at once.

Once upon a time
never-ending rhythms
of joy and affection
engulfed in buttered limbs.

Arm me with the grit needed to
withstand the grief of rejection
with a sprinkle of humiliation.

Humility minus the salt
(don't be too salty sis)
plus light sugar
(because sugar coating is never ok)
plus self-improvement

MMMmmm, a nice slice of humble pie.

Should I

The facade of contentment fades.
The shade has created a permanent sleep
from which I wish not to awake.
An occasional rumble of hunger entices me to taste
life again.
What is left to partake once the dinner party ends?
Let me regurgitate old scenes and let me be.

Drive

Slowing down, savoring
move too fast just laboring

Ease thru life unwavering
energy wasted detangling

Absorbing each droplet
gushing and flooding

Denounce the popular path
or hit that traffic and crash.

Motivation

I AM NEVER ENOUGH
GOTTA BE TOUGH.
AM NEVER ENOUGH
DON'T BE TOO ROUGH
NEVER ENOUGH
KNOW HOW TO TOUCH
SHHH...ENOUGH
DON'T SAY TO MUCH.
ENOUGH NEVER AM I?
DON'T ACCEPT FAILURE, ALWAYS TRY.
NEVER AM I?
DON'T LET THEM SEE YOU CRY
AM I?
REMEMBERED AFTER I DIE?
I...
ENOUGH? ENOUGH!

Job

Push away my pride
what you want I'll abide
What you need tell me now
give a f**k why, when, and how
Just let me know
I'll go with the flow
of this something
of this nothing
of this loving
of this f*****g
sheesh!
there I go again
trying to tell you how it's gonna go
steady telling you how it has been
and you exclaim "Shut up and let me dive in!"
Damn why does it have to be this way?
All I ever want is for you to want me to stay.
And since I'm not beautiful and do not slay
I say "Ok" and get to it.
Imagining a romantic version of you and this
scene
but in reality your hoe.

Showtime

Struggling to create a life envisioned before time.
Ethereal beings gaze upon our spirits in confusion
concerned about the future dimensions but laughing
at our pain.
Why bother to change what will happen since the
lines are arranged, the roles are rehearsed, and the
future is set?
Lights, camera, action.

Win

The wrong battles have been won.
The significant wars lost. I have claimed victory
many a time but at what cost?
Obviously my livelihood and beauty have
escaped me.
My strength has transformed into ripples,
chunks, and lumps.
My agility has stretched thin and disappeared.
My even tone has burned and faded in all the
wrong places.
Disease has become insatiable, lurking until I
sleep.
Spirit hold strong because my mind and body
cannot keep a foothold but you still blaze within
and for this reason
I just may live to win again.

Content

Unanswered questions create chaos or chemistry?
Either way my choices may be the death of me.
Wreaking havoc in my mind, on my body, and
through my soul.
Outcomes and consequences which silently swirl out
of control.
Behold, the mixing bowl of lies and deceit
have created distrust and now peace is all I seek.
No need to explain, the will to fight is gone,
so many tears have washed away the pain
and I'm content with just silence at home.
Work is stressful but finding a new career...doubtful.
Aiming to please has left me with boring
conversation and bad knees.
Oh but don't you feel bad for me because all the
exciting memories that led me here are forevermore.

Questions

How many more generations are left to endure this treacherous cycle of death? Who or what watches us with curiosity as we create more babies to feed that either become animals or victims of monstrosity? How many more geniuses will be allowed to share their knowledge while others waste money and time in college? Does nature surround us and serve as spies for the higher being who decides who dies? Are there those around us who have mastered their brain activity and therefore thrive? Are humans so selfish that we will never cure homelessness and hunger? Is God really laughing at human beings' blunders...is that the sound of thunder?

Trees

They grow up and down, out and around until they seem to surround the entire being of me. Creating synonymous patterns with splotches of ragged edges begging to be filed and smoothed so as to fit more perfectly within this false reality. Shades of green and blue have withered into yellow, creeping steadily to decayed browns and grey. The limbs constantly sway, teasing me with the chance of breaking due to the extensive decay. Occasionally gazing up as I reach to the sky hoping the prize will place itself before my eyes.

Last One

Three times before I knew not what was in store and cowardly denied the gift growing inside. A fourth time the joke is on me as we tried to reach three for the Almighty decided it was time for me to suffer and learn my lesson. A life of sin had caught up with me and I could no longer runaway from the fading timeline. But here comes my blessing as a reminder that I have not been forsaken and there just may be enough time for me to right my wrongs and provide a safe haven for the next generation.

School

13

Abandoned by mother, mishandled by father, distrusted by grandma, pitied by grandpa. A cousin to call brother because his mother was not ready, someone she could relate to because neither had a daddy. Threatened and beaten almost daily but that's how they were raised and it did create the habit of getting all A's so I guess that s**t was ok. Wish she could have stayed but when Daddy decided to try it ended with seeing fiends get high and a man ripping away my age to leave behind a bruised behind and a mindset of thinking nobody else taking what is mine. Being book smart and street smart is the necessary rule to live this life she lived and all this was achieved before middle school.

Truth

If I only had known the truth behind the spotlight and the shades of sunshine and airy whispers of delight. Someone should have warned me of the multilayered tiers of grief and tears combined with thickened skin creating this building of walls which now resemble one-way mirrors and I the spectacle. Surely one had the notion to scream out "beware" or "don't go there" but instead what was witnessed were stares as I climbed the stairwell. Correction... descended into the well only to plummet into cold darkness mixed with hot flashes of hell with only myself to blame for the pain, ashamed. Well let me have a drink, indulge a little of this, swallow a little of that while I am here right? No need to cower with no consequences in sight and die down here, I just might. So many to accompany me so my pity, anger, and fright have vanished. I promise to remain silent even through the anguish.

Hate

15

Hate is an awful, unnecessary word they say. I disagree because hate means to you not what it means to me. HONOR the value of your enemies for without them what would you be? Simply another face and body of matter caught in the mundane iniquity bearing world. Someone lingers that proves your relevancy. ALL of them not some of them can feel this heat that spews through clenched teeth or sometimes the prize is a cut of the eyes, I will not lie. THINE that are chosen have openly shown their purpose to harm whether spoken or concealed with charm or have already felt the strength of my arms. Enemies come and go, friends may become foe although an honorable life is the goal. Just know although I egress peacefully I choose Hate - Honor All Thine Enemies so I can be free.

Bloodstream

A path of forgotten memories and somber traumas.
Shades of pink with love, hope, and comfort. Hues of
bright red distorted pain and sadness. Stains of black,
dull moments of pure anger, revenge, and violence.
This moisture feels too familiar. Decades of wading
aimlessly in lakes, feeling trapped in ponds,
searching for land in oceans before realizing I had
ventured too far. Ripping the drenched clothes from
my body until I am naked; unwilling to go on.
Robotic movements gravitate to drying the trail by
removing all evidence...smiling as if all is well.
Droplets of tears have escalated to another tragedy.
As long as life flows without pooling into a cesspool
of clots, remaining a bloodstream, I will become
clean of all toxicity and learn to love me.

First Son

Your purpose was to stop me from my ongoing insanity of repeated passions with no end goal in sight. No plan with daddy just someone to fulfill my physical needs instead of laying with random guys and taking flight. He made me feel important and as if I was a prize. Once I became pregnant it were as if I'd lost my eyes. Playing house and making demands and both of us confused. Poor daddy made out to feel like an aggressor and a dog by outsiders when he was just doing what boys that age should do. He had not made any commitments and I was playing myself but you my dear showed up to help. You provided me focus and a will to not feel pitiful. You did not ruin my body so I could still feel beautiful. Prepared me to understand difficult decisions must be made. Ignited self-awareness and that I needed to change. Although my transformation took awhile and another child to occur, the path you funneled for me provided the map for my journey. You are my first born son.

Love lost

I take responsibility for you falling out of love with me. Although we both know that your ego won in the fight of love vs lust. The thrusts you gave me time and time again grew weaker and less passionate so let's look within. I failed to show improvement in all I said and did with the exception of discontinuing knocking tramps upside their heads. I had an energy and lost some weight but loneliness and too much self time continued to load my plate. The fault does not belong to you for you're a man and have feelings too. I understand that my haughtiness offends the very ground that surrounds you and presents embarrassment amongst your family and colleagues too. So I grant you your freedom please enjoy those females if you need them. What's that cliche; if you cannot join them, lead them.

Do Not Touch

19

What is the point of flowers that bloom if only to wither and die without attention and devotion. Such expectations prove deadly, such emotions exude careless disregard of truths forever hidden by the bees and the trees. Onlookers provide temporary pleasures, nature seekers give interested glances only to continue without touching or uprooting to places unknown with the guarantee of providing unrequited love. Let them be. Allow the joy of lonely pastures never to endure the rights of passage that lead to paths of destruction...do not touch them.

My Light

Be all I was never could never and will never be. Disregard my viewed and spoken hesitancies so as to proceed with caution nonetheless. Uttered wariness is spoken by the fright within, shut out the need to impress mother dearest because she does not know best. You are the light, proven to be the lead. I take no responsibility, at best perhaps planted a seed by exhibiting who and what to avoid and dodge the life of void. Love to live without living to love, hug. Establish some boundaries and keep your word. Protect your peace and separate with ease. Adore yourself, fight for you please.

End It

Thoughts of revelation never expressed
Visions of joy the toy never bought
Instances of relief a mere belief
now airy inspirations for the spirits and demons
to end it.

www.ingramcontent.com/pod-product-compliance
Lightning Source LLC
Chambersburg PA
CBHW071246140726
47996CB00007B/2775